How To Manage Money

Because Everything You Believe To Be True About Money Is False, And Because There Are Clever Methods To Increase Your Income

(The Definitive Guide To Financial Independence)

Rolando Mullen

TABLE OF CONTENT

Advantages Of Financial Management............................ 1
Are You Read? 8
How Compound Interest Affects A Budget................13
Why You Can't Develop Your Money Management Techniques 23
Some More Advice 53
Making Purchasing Choices 64
Debt Management Techniques................................74
Finders Keepers..86
Save More Money...93
Guidelines For Managing Your Money Flow.............98
Get Your Finances In Order 102
How To Maintain Focus...117
Money Management Best Tips 122

Advantages Of Financial Management

When you consistently earn a large income, whether it comes from a high salary, investments in successful businesses, or both, there is a considerable probability that you will overspend and run out of money at the end of the month. Such wasteful expenditure is avoided via wealth management, which also enables you to increase your savings. You may easily accomplish your objectives without running out of money by saving more money.

Possessing sound money management techniques has several advantages. If you are able to handle your money well, you will open up new doors in life that were previously closed off by a lack of funds. A life without constraints is now within your grasp thanks to good money management abilities. The advantages listed below are some of the things you may get by managing your money well.

Your Money Streamlined:

You can simply control the inflows and outflows of your money if you create a budget and adhere to it. This is highly beneficial since it makes it simple to pinpoint the areas where your expenditure is higher and, eventually, helps you discover strategies to save costs. With time, you may change and improve your money for numerous areas, including retirement, vacation, and savings accounts.

Maintains Your Focus on Your Financial Objectives:

You may cut down on spending on goods and services that don't improve your present financial situation by using sound money management techniques. When resources are few and options are many, good money management makes it simpler to get by. You may order your objectives and concentrate on the most crucial ones.

enables you to earn more money:

You may really earn more money if you handle your money well. You create a budget where you may find and get rid of unnecessary costs. If you manage your finances, you won't have any extra spending on things like late fees, penalties, and interest. All of these little sums of money saved over time might boost your overall financial situation.

Live a Life Free of tension: You may live a life free of tension by handling your money well. Money is undoubtedly the most stressful element in a person's life, thus it is crucial to handle it precisely in order to avoid or drastically lessen the tension it causes. If you don't have enough money, it will be difficult for you to pay your bills on time or for things like your children's college tuition. You will not only enjoy life more if you have some extra money set away, but you will also feel lot safer. A key part in lowering stress is really played by pleasure and security. Therefore, learning money management skills is essential if you want to have a stress-free life.

Fulfill Your Dreams

Everyone aspires to live out their aspirations. Everybody has various ambitions, and virtually all of them include money in some capacity. If your ambition involves money in any way, managing your money well is the only way to make it a reality. You won't be able to achieve your goals if you don't improve your money management abilities. You'll find it difficult to get your companion on the holidays of their dreams. But if you manage your money well, ideal holidays are more attainable. This is only a little illustration of how everything is possible. If you have enough money, you may not have a problem sending your kids to college. Similar to this, you may fulfill your child's wish to see his preferred professional sports team in person. In a nutshell, we can say that all of your dreams are dependent on your financial situation; if you have money, you can realize your ambitions, but if you don't manage it, you'll always run into problems.

Most individuals desire to travel and take vacations, so they learn how to manage their money in order to do so. You'll be in a better position to enjoy your holidays and travel more if you have solid money management abilities. The most expensive pastimes are traveling and seeing the globe. If you want to visit the whole globe, you must pay close attention to your spending and earning patterns. You can only take a vacation and travel the globe if you have a lot of money.

Your Ultimate Freedom and Money are Related

The degree of freedom a person has in their everyday life in this materialistic environment is influenced by their financial situation. The more money you have, the more wishes you can fulfill. You actually can accomplish practically whatever you want if you have enough money. You may have greater independence if you develop excellent money management abilities. You can travel the globe and have a free life thanks to the money you have.

Debt is not a concern:

You may get out of debt fairly quickly if you understand how to manage your money, stay on track with your goals, and create a budget. When you manage your money correctly, you'll be able to pay off all of your debts on time and reduce your reliance on them. Furthermore, if you include student loan payments in your budget, depression won't be a result of them.

Take Nothing for Granted:

Regardless of how much money you make or how safe you feel in your present position, the future is unpredictable, and the current economic climate might alter your financial situation. If you have been managing your money well, you can overcome obstacles and be prepared for tough economic times. You have emergency money, so surviving through difficult times won't be a problem for you. Therefore, wise money management may help you deal with unforeseen circumstances.

Are You Read?

The title of this article may be confusing to you, but you are obviously ready because you are reading it. Although that is technically the truth, many people do get into situations where they are unsure of whether they will follow through or not. If you aren't prepared to manage your money, you won't take the essential steps to do so. So to start, in my opinion, it is always wise to be aware of your situation and consider certain indicators that may indicate that you should start managing your finances. There are unmistakable indicators that you need to manage your finances, adopt a new system, or just learn something new to assist you. We will go through a couple of them in this chapter, not only to point them out but also to help you identify any potential mistakes you may be making so you can fix them later.

1. You have no understanding where your money is going Prior to learning

how to handle my money, I had no idea what I was spending it on. But once I began in charge of it, I understood the issue. I was out of control with my spending and had no goals for my money, so I spent on impulse (mainly shopping).

Since I've Began Managing It, I've Become More Perceptive, and I've Even Went As Far As To Hire Someone To File My Receipts, Which Gives Me A Detailed Overview Of When And Exactly What I Spend On. If you too encounter this issue, it is important to begin controlling it so that you can see where it is headed and how to take control of it.

2. A last month to extend the money

If you see that you run out of money before taking care of all that is necessary, you should start learning better money management techniques. Because of this, it may indicate that you often make impulsive purchases or that you just need to simplify your life a little.

Both of which are possible with the appropriate financial understanding.

3. It's unpleasant

Consider it in this manner If someone inquired about your brand-new automobile, you would react with a chirp and a grin. Yet, what do you say when the topic of money is raised? Does it thrill you, make you joyful, make you want to change the topic, or do you experience dread? If so, there must be something about your money that you dislike.

I used to despise the subject as well, but I later realized that my frustration wasn't with the money per such, but rather with how I was handling it. The bills were out of balance, and they were losing money and sometimes giving too much out. But after I managed to control it, I began to really like discussing it and get fired up about managing it.

4. You go to work, eat, sleep, and pay bills every day in order to survive. These days, it seems like it is the only thing you do with your money. However, I discovered a few years ago that the true reason you aren't producing enough money is because your system doesn't create many other plans. Yes, the bills may seem to be everything, but as you have greater control over your finances, your costs will eventually decrease and you will begin spending less and less on them.

If you often miss payments, fear that your card will be refused, carry credit card balances over, incur frequent overdraft penalties, and have less than $100 in your bank account, your finances are a major cause of stress. then undoubtedly something is wrong, and it's time to adopt a fresh outlook and new routines. You cannot address a problem with the same mentality that caused it, a great thinker once stated. Only fresh information, experience, and wisdom may be used to resolve them. Money need not just be a source of worry; it can also be a source of great joy.

There you have it. If you feel that you have seen enough and are ready to go on to developing better money management habits after reading the previous page, then let's continue.

How Compound Interest Affects A Budget

The act of reinvesting an asset to generate a bigger yield is known as "compound interest."

There must be two components for it to work. One of them is reinvested time and profits. One of the most potent investing strategies known, compound interest may help an original investment grow tremendously. The phrase is not brand-new in the financial world; the idea is nothing new. Capitalization was recognized as one of the most significant financial concepts by Warren Buffet and Benjamin Graham, and it was termed the "eighth wonder of the world" by Albert Einstein.

According to Warren Buffet in one of his letters to his investing partners, it is the most effective technique for generating wealth via investments.

Capitalization is the process of reinjecting investment returns into the cycle to produce more returns. The outcomes have produced a snowball effect, with the portfolio expanding quickly the longer it goes without reinvesting. On the other hand, capitalization needs time and care. Many contemporary investors who live in a fast-paced atmosphere are alarmed by these items.

When it comes to money management, the potential rewards are larger the more risk a person is ready to accept. Stock investment gives longer-term profits that are better than savings account investing. Many consumers had a risk allergy after the start of the financial crisis in 2008, and they decided to accept fewer profits in order to lessen the risk. Money is secure in a standard savings account, but the profits on such an investment may not be sufficient to keep up with inflation, which is the issue. Regular savings accounts are required for emergencies, but investing in higher-risk ventures may improve the outlook for long-term finances.

Despite how alluring it may seem, you must resist the temptation to increase your risks in order to reap more profits. You'll be motivated to take the necessary steps to get a greater rate of return, which could be as high as 20%, after just one glance at the compound interest table for the cash you choose to invest. This may be rather hazardous in the long term. No matter how successful the firm is in its early phases, you need to take precautions to prevent the possibility of going bankrupt before you know what you're doing. In the early stages of the financial industry, returns of 20-60% are very respectable, but if there is a possibility of 80-100% negative returns someplace, it will be the end of the world since all the money will be lost and there would be no more. Profits cannot be made in any form.

advantages of compound interest
Many consumers and company owners struggle to control variations in cash flow. A corporation may be able to maintain its profitability over the long

run with even a little portion of money saved and invested in a compound interest structure. On the other side, accumulating too much debt in such an account can result in future monetary issues.

The notion

If a business deposits 10,000 euros in an account, it will earn interest on both the principal amount and the profit generated by the total interest.

a practical perspective

The more the money benefits the company over time, the longer it remains in the compounding account. The amount of advantage compounding offers depends significantly on how often interest is compounded. Compared to investments that compound quarterly or even monthly, yearly investments are likely to increase more slowly over time.

advantages of saving

Understanding the concept of compound interest may help you save money and increase the amount of money you can make investments with. Compound interest is used to compute interest if the firm uses credit cards often and does not pay the whole debt each month.

Purchasing dividends

The investor has a choice of options for reinvestment. Reinvesting dividends is advantageous for firms and corporations. This is not a stock DRIP. The ability to withdraw dividends and reinvest them with more funds may ultimately boost profitability.

In terms of dividends, compound interest may also be benefited in various ways.

The real story behind compound interest

Compound interest is one of the most effective methods for building money.

What does compound interest's "snowball effect" imply to you? If you've ever invested money, it's probable that you were given figures to help you picture how your investment would develop over time.

These figures may have been taken from a flier, an artwork, or even a spreadsheet projection. It's possible that you did some calculations on your own since it's thrilling to think about the advantages that our work will have in the future.

We can demonstrate that if you have 100,000 euros to invest, your money will grow to over one million euros after 30 years at an annual interest rate of 8%.

Or maybe you wish to start contributing to your employer's retirement plan and choose a $10,000 yearly commitment. 1,006,265.69 precisely. A $10,000 investment would grow to roughly $1 million over 30 years at an annual return rate of 8%. (That is $1,223,458.68 for those of you who want to be accurate.) This appears to be an obvious choice. Though is it?

Sadly, there are a number of obstacles that will prevent you from receiving that million over the following 30 years. Though technically sound, these figures only provide a partial picture of the situation.

The most crucial point, which we are never informed of, is that nothing can prevent compound interest from operating to its full potential. As soon as there is a break, all bets are off.

The most crucial point, which we are never informed of, is that nothing can prevent compound interest from operating to its full potential. And by that, I mean nothing. As soon as there is a break, however little, all bets are off.

The outcomes are unexpectedly different.

Examples include account fees, taxes on profits, investment losses, and purchases made with invested money.

Compound interest does not continue to grow when a loss occurs.

We are often taught that taking risks is necessary if we are to achieve major advantages. Is this a fact? Think about it: given everything we've talked so far, would you choose to take a stable 9.25% return every year or take a chance on certain losses in exchange for the chance to sometimes make returns as high as 20% and even 30%?

Let's take a new approach to this. You would only need to earn 7.46% interest on your $100,000 investment for 19 years in order to make the same $390,000 by investing in the stock market from 1997 to 2015. That indicates that just included losses in the equation decreased your return by about two percentage points.

Do your investments have fees? There is no question that there exist. Particularly when it comes to stock market investment, fees are unavoidable. Day traders must pay for their deals as well. We must, however, pay extra fees since the majority of us are not day traders. Fees for management, mutual funds, and the purchase and sale of stocks and bonds are a few examples.

Compound interest stops compounding after fees are applied to our account.

What happens to your compound interest when fees are withdrawn from your account balance each year? Start by thinking about the parallels between a charge and a loss. It's a defeat, let's face it. Even a little setback still counts as a loss.

And in a few respects, that loss will be distinct from a market loss. Do you know what that distinction is?

Our anticipated account balance has increased from $540,000 to $390,000, losses included. The increase falls from $390,000 to $267,252 if we add a 2% yearly charge to the investment throughout these 19 years (the $267,252 amount will be rounded to $270,000 in the following sentences).

Compound interest stops growing after we pay taxes on our gains.

We started by estimating that $100,000 would increase to $540,000 in 19 years if invested at a 9.25% annual return rate. Our account lost money four times in 19 years, bringing the total down to $390,000. Even though we still generated an average return of 9.25% throughout this time, our compounding curve was broken by four years of losses, and the momentum that was lost could not be entirely regained. Due to expenditures, our total has now dropped to $270,000, meaning that we have now spent $440,000 of our $540,000 initial budget.

Are you starting to comprehend why, at this time in your life, your personal

investments are not performing as you had hoped? Do not lose heart.
Understanding is a useful tool. You will be set free by the truth.

Why You Can't Develop Your Money Management Techniques

You may first believe that you are progressing. But let's think about investing the same time and effort into practicing the piano for the sake of comparison. Would your skill level in each after performing these tasks for a few hours every week, let's say, over the course of a few months, be comparable? Maybe.

Let's make that time period a year long. What would you now be doing on the piano in comparison to your money management efforts? What about five years from now? By this time, you may easily be doing feats of magic with that pianist.

How are your money management skills and productivity level? Are you still keeping track of that loose change on your mobile app after each cup of coffee you purchase? At this point, you may realize that your skill level and productivity won't ever significantly increase, regardless of how many more years of time and effort you devote to "practicing" money management.

There is only one explanation for why your personal financial management proficiency and productivity have long since been established while your level of piano playing skills continues to rise.

Figuratively and literally, when learning to play the piano (or learning to manage your money), you must first map out where all the notes are on the keyboard (or where all the money is in your life) to gain an understanding of what is ahead of you before you can start playing your first two-finger tune (or actually starting to manage your money). But

Here is where your piano playing talent breaks out and your money management abilities go by the wayside.

Without giving it a second thought, you would assume that all the notes on the keyboard were in the same location as they were the first time you played the piano. Naturally, with "practice" (doing the same thing again; this is an important difference), you may remember the positions of the notes and go to the next level, practicing managing those notes while you really perform the song.

Contrarily, while managing your money for the second time, you must first determine where all of your notes are since they have all moved since the last time you "practiced" (timeframes, income, expenses, balances, etc.). You could realize that the only thing you are practicing at this stage is discovering notes.

The truth is that if you continue to manage your money in this manner, you will always have a brand-new keyboard layout (financial picture) in front of you.

In actuality, you are beginning over each and every time. This is the reason why you can't improve your money management abilities to the same degree that you can improve your piano playing abilities.

Turn this idea around. After five years, how good would you be at playing the same simple tune on that piano if each time you sat down to play it, you had to first find out where all the notes were? Perhaps you were aware of the issue right away, leading you to choose to use the most recent, very sophisticated note-finding software. But how are you doing?

level are you really playing the song at? Improving? How soon, say, five years from now?

You might realize that no matter how well you honed your note-finding skills, your performance threshold has never truly advanced and will never do so because your grasp of the key concepts (your financial picture) will always be constrained because it is never the same.

But now consider what may happen to the whole idea of money management if your money (timeframes, income, expenses, balances, etc.) remained in exactly the same position as you left it the last time...and the time before that. If you want to get a decent idea of what that experience would be like, think about what occurs to a musician when their level of proficiency at playing increases.

such piano.

Consider the fact that a musician may quickly stop thinking about the notes on the keyboard (can you imagine?). The musician's first efforts to "account" for the notes (pun intended) have naturally advanced to the organization and management of the notes (singing playing/money management). His song playing becomes more complicated and precise with time while also becoming easier and less labor-intensive via simple repetition and memory. His understanding of the keyboard has evolved into a completely intuitive state (invisible?), and he is now working at a higher pace, doing more with the barest amount of effort.

Paragraph 2

Making A Successful Personal Budget

Budgeting always comes up when people are talking about managing their finances. Despite popular belief, "budgeting" is the most useful tool there is for managing finances. Even though sticking to a budget is a wise financial habit, most people find it unpleasant. We like following the crowd, especially when it comes to money, for some reason. While many see it as an additional burden, others associate budgeting with not being able to fully enjoy life. They don't realize it, but one of the things that might lead to the much-desired financial independence is budgeting.

Why is budgeting so crucial?

Budgeting provides additional advantages that many of us fail to see, in addition to the promise of financial independence. First of all, it provides you financial control. You will have complete discretion over where and how you spend your hard-earned money. I can hear you saying that you want to live life on your terms. Even on a limited budget, you can. Maybe you'll have to give up your daily cup of pricey coffee, but at the end of the month, you get to take a trip somewhere exotic. It's a tiny price to pay for a significant gain. Without a budget, you may grant your modest requests but not your larger, more expensive ones.

Another reason why budgeting is crucial is that it keeps your attention on your longer-term financial objectives. You could one day wish to establish a side company, for instance, but you'll need money for that. You may accumulate the cash via budgeting over time. Budgeting also helps if your goal is just to make ends meet. You won't run out of money at the end of the month to cover your essential expenses.

For individuals who are struggling with debt, it is a lifesaver. Knowing your income and outgoing expenses is made easier with a budget. Calculating how much money you should set aside to pay off all of your obligations is simple.

Additionally, it helps you assess your financial situation and decide if you can take on additional debt. It provides you a better understanding of your optimum debt amount depending on your financial situation, one that will benefit you and prevent you from getting into further trouble in the future.

Most significantly, however, it makes it easier for you to talk to your loved ones and significant other about money. It might be a means for you to demonstrate to everyone that you have objectives to achieve and how you should all allocate the limited resources. When there are expectations from your loved ones, money may become a source of contention. But by clearly outlining how much is accessible and how you must collectively utilize it as a team, this dispute may be avoided.

How can I create a personal spending plan?

The subject of how to create a budget plan still exists if you are willing to stick to it. There are many factors to take into consideration while creating your initial budget plan, which may be fairly intimidating. You may use the following guidance to make the process of creating a budget a snap.

Determine how much money you already have in your possession as a first step. Checking all of your savings, checking, and investment accounts is part of this. You also need to be aware of the costs and interest rates associated with each of the accounts you utilize. The sum of all these numbers will be your net worth.

Your monthly income is the next item you should record. It shouldn't be an issue for you if your salary is stable, but if it varies each month, you may record your average income for the previous 12 months.

You may go on from this step if you have no debts. However, if you have debt, you must record the monthly payments. How do you do that? Calculate your total debt and the required minimum payment. Include all of your bills, including credit card balances, auto loans, school loans, and mortgages. Avoid missing anything!

It's time for you to ultimately determine your net worth after gathering all of those information. An easy computation is required:

Total assets minus all debts equals net worth.

Simply put, your net worth is the amount that remains after deducting all of your assets from your liabilities. And if your net worth is negative, don't be shocked. Beginners often have negative net worth. Particularly among those who have just begun their professions and are almost certainly carrying hefty college debt.

You should also figure out how much you typically spend each month on necessities. This one might be difficult to estimate, but if you look at your receipts and invoices from the previous month, you can get close.

You may do the remaining budgeting tasks manually if you'd like. However, there are several programs available today that may even create a long-term, sustainable financial plan for you. To create your own budget, you may always depend on programs like Mint, Mvelopes, or even Microsoft Excel.

When you review your budget plan, you'll know if you need to make changes to lower your spending or whether you're already managing your money well. Whatever the situation, keep in mind that increasing your income is the key to winning this financial conflict. Therefore, keep an eye out for chances and work to boost your revenue.

If your net worth is positive, you should use this money to start a savings account; if it is negative, you will need to reduce a few costs. can use this money to invest in anything to make more money.

Finally, keep track of your finances and stick to your financial plan. While creating and sticking to a budget can annoy you at first, as time goes on, you'll realize how crucial it is to reap the bigger pleasures in life. You will have a greater understanding of how to manage your finances in the next chapter. Continue reading to learn some of the complex facts you need to maximize your financial gains.

A GUIDE TO BEGINNING MONEY MANAGEMENT

The way you handle, spend, and invest your money may have a significant influence on your life, yet relatively few educational institutions teach these crucial skills. Financial savvy might be difficult to learn, but the fundamentals are quite straightforward and never change. Here is where to start.

You probably learned some fundamental math when you were growing up, but far too many people make it all the way to adulthood without ever learning basic money management. Skills like budgeting, investing for the future, or even understanding how credit cards work are astonishingly common. If you need a Money 101, we'll go over the fundamentals while also providing you with the tools you need to learn more.

Guidelines for Personal Finance

Managing your finances seems like a lot of paper work and numbers. You earn X dollars, you spend Y dollars, and you make an effort to ensure that Y is less than X. However, your money are just as much a reflection of your psychology, habits, and beliefs that you decide to live by. In other words, your mindset is just as important as the math.

- Spend less than you earn: If your income is $30,000 per ycar and your expenses are $31,000, you will find it difficult to escape a debt cycle. You won't be ready for emergencies or significant life changes if you spend exactly what you make each year. Spending less than you make gives you the freedom to save, plan for the future, and handle the inevitable difficulties that life will throw your way. The greater the difference between your income and spending, the better.

- Always make plans for the future; this doesn't only refer to retirement. If a store offers to let you pay off a device in six months with no interest, you need to be aware that you may do so in order to avoid the deal. Establishing an emergency fund can enable you to deal with unforeseen auto repairs or medical expenses. If you have a retirement plan, you can be confident you will have income if you are unable to work any longer. Your finances should always look beyond the current month.

- Make your money earn more money: Curious about how the wealthy keep becoming richer? Because money may grow while you sleep if you save part of it. Money that is well invested grows in value over time. Don't just deposit all of your money in a low-interest savings account. Invest in items that will make you more money than you did before. Sometimes that's an investment account, but other times it's starting a business or even pursuing schooling in order to get a better-paying position.

The most crucial personal financial laws remain constant. What your grandparents did may not be effective for you. To manage your money, newer, better tools will always be available. Spending less than you make will always be beneficial, however. It will always be better to invest your money than to do nothing with it. Furthermore, making plans for the future is always preferable than spending your paycheque as soon as you get it.

Finding a Bank Account

It's neither safe nor advisable to keep all of your money in your wallet. To keep track of your spending money and short-term savings, you'll need some form of account. Your money may be held by a bank (or credit union) and accessible using an ATM or debit card. Opening a bank account is simple. You may often apply online or visit a branch and ask a teller to create an account; they will walk you through the procedure. Picking a bank is more difficult.

Finding a bank means locating a company that offers the services you want at the lowest possible cost. Debit cards, ATM access (or at the at least, refunding fees for using other banks' ATMs), paper checks, and a website where you can check your account balance are examples of common services. There are many worthwhile banks that don't need you to meet any of these conditions, even if some charge monthly fees or mandate that you maintain a minimum balance. We've spoken more about what to look for in a bank here.

Chances are, most of the adults in your life have recommendations for which bank they favor. However, the FDIC has a tool here that you may use to search for insured banks in your area if you can't get a good suggestion. The website can locate bakeries close to you and, where available, provide links to those businesses' websites. Another wonderful online tool that compares checking accounts from various banks is available here from Nerd Wallet.

Of course, keep in mind that not all banks have actual doors. Some banks, like Simple, Ally, or Capital One 360, only accept payments online. These sometimes include trade-offs (such as, you know, not having physical branches), but many provide lower fees and better services. Additionally, they often provide higher interest rates than traditional banks, meaning that the money you save will earn a little extra money just by being in your account. This is because they incur less operating expenses than traditional banks since they don't own physical buildings.

Once you've chosen a bank, either visit the company's website or a nearby branch and request to open a new account. To prove that you are who you say you are, you will need to provide basic forms of identification such your name, social security number, birthdate, and some kind of photo ID like a driver's license. You may check with the bank you want for specifics by doing so.

Do you know where your money goes, or does it just seem to vanish from your account? Even a simple, barebones budget is one of the best ways to ensure that you are spending less than you earn, so getting a head start is crucial. You don't have much money when you're young and your profession is just getting started. Developing the habit of classifying your bills and keeping track of your expenses might help you avoid many financial issues before they ever arise. If you're creating a budget for the first time, it may be simpler to start with paper, a pen, and a calculator, but we'll get to more sophisticated tools you can use in a moment.

Start by figuring out how much money you earn every month. If you are paid by the hour, multiply your salary by the standard number of hours you work each month. Then, list all of your regular expenses in writing. This includes ongoing expenses like your rent or mortgage, utilities, auto payments, and so on. You may need to keep track of your spending over time for more complex items like food. If paper work isn't your thing, gather together your receipts from the last several weeks or use your bank's transaction history. Estimate while waiting for an exact number if you can. Keep track of all of your expenses over the following month or two. Add everything up at the end of each month to see how much you are spending in each category.

Your monthly expenses should ideally be less than your monthly income. If it isn't, start going over your list to see which expenses you can reduce until it is. Cut brutally if necessary. For some, it can be as simple as cutting those pastries, but for others, you might need to decide if you can afford to live in that pricey city.

Once you've gotten the hang of keeping track of your costs, you may try using a service like Mint to handle it for you. You can simply see how much you're spending on bills, groceries, restaurants, shopping, and other categories by connecting your bank account, which will automatically categorize your transactions. You may use it to create budgets for various things, such as groceries or entertainment, and get alerted when you're going over. More information on how to use Mint may be found in our beginner's guide.

You've developed the habit of tracking your spending, now it's time to create that budget. Here, there are a few different philosophies. Some people want to have a very detailed history of their travels, complete with strict allotments for expenses like food, clothing, and entertainment. Others, such as financial expert Ramit Sethi, think that being too rigorous is ineffective. Instead, Sethi advises segmenting your finances into the following four groups:

Fixated costs (50–60%): This should include any cost that you are aware will occur each month and that seldom changes. Rent, gas, electricity, food, your phone bill, and everything else that often remains the same are included. Some of them may change somewhat from month to month, but they are still necessary for regular life and at least fairly predictable.

Investments (10%): As you accumulate your savings (which we'll cover later), you'll ultimately want to invest some of your money so that it increases over time. You may account for any investments, such as a company 401(k), that are deducted from your paycheck here.

Short- and long-term savings should fall under this category (5–10%). This includes setting aside money for trips, gifts, or significant purchases like a new TV or computer. You should also add an emergency fund in this category, which is just a sum of money kept in a savings account for unforeseen expenses like car repairs or unexpected expenditures.

Guilt-free Spending (20–35%): You may include anything in this category. Although eating out, drinking, or spending money on entertainment is sometimes regarded as a financial advantage, the fact is that we really do these things because we like them. As long as the other three categories are taken care of, you may spend this money without feeling guilty about your spending plan.

These are Sethi's recommendations for young people, but you may (and should) modify the percentages based on your age, your financial goals, and the things that are important to you. Remember that the more money you save, the more you'll have later to buy a home, retire early, or accomplish other goals. (We'll discuss more about this later.)

Budgeting really just entails knowing where your money is going and making plans for the future. This plan will still cover the most of what you need to budget for if you don't want to deal with the hassle of keeping track of every each penny you spend at the gas station. The only decision you need to make is how much you will place in each category. We have included Sethi's recommended percentages as a reference, but you are free to modify as necessary. Save what you can if you are unable to set aside or invest 10% of your income after expenses. Instead of forcing yourself to spend 20% of your budget on vices, you may increase your savings. The more you can put aside, the better.

Starting long-term investments will often be one of the hardest stages of your financial life since, when you're just getting started, you don't have much money. For that reason, it's crucial that you review your investments if you get a raise or a new job that pays you more. It's tempting to upgrade your life with a new vehicle, apartment, or pricey toys to fit your new budget when you start to make more money. While it's okay to move up, there will never be a better moment to boost your long-term savings than when you're already living on a lesser budget than you're earning. This is what's known as "lifestyle inflation."

Earned Income Section

Money you get from your employment is considered earned income. which you then use to maintain your lifestyle and make purchases on a regular basis. Living a full and happy life vs one that is fraught with uncertainty and concern that you won't be able to pay your payments depends on making the most of that money and prudent judgments. Your earned income is what you will use to pay your expenses, save money, and subsist on a daily basis. It goes without saying that the more money you make, the more you can put toward both your bills and your own needs and goals. Your capacity to save money and afterwards invest it will be mostly fueled by your capacity to generate income.

Your lifestyle, your family's lifestyle, and the options available to you and your family will all be influenced by the amount of money you earn, so picking your method of earning is crucial. You should have a job or profession that you like and that also supports you financially. Only you can decide what is best for you in this situation; sometimes that means waiting 10 years after graduating from high school or college. You must consider your alternatives and decide whether your time is worth what they are prepared to pay you since, if you work for a corporation or business, you will be exchanging your time for money.

When picking a job, it's crucial to exercise caution since some occupations have a 30-year lifespan. If that's not your cup of tea, you could choose to become an entrepreneur. As such, you must be prepared for it to be very chaotic and sporadic, and your income may fluctuate at times. However, as an entrepreneur, you may find success and financial independence much more quickly than those who depend on an employer to compensate them for their labor. Find a profession and a passion you like, take that money, and utilize it to invest wisely and provide your family financial stability and independence, is advice given by many successful businesspeople.

Some company owners, like Grant Cardone, have been successful in transferring money from their occupations to their enterprises and then investing it all to amass a large net worth. In order to construct an investing pot, Grant Cardone saved and pooled all of his earned income. From there, he would direct all of his funds into investments. When he ran out of money, he would try that approach once again to locate another investment. Therefore, this straightforward plan of earning an income, saving, and then investing helped establish a net worth of over $300 million, which is growing year. Grant's plan is to increase his net worth by combining his earned income with investment flows. There will come a time when your investment income will enable you to live the life of your dreams, even if it may start off slowly.

The turning moment is when you have put in a lot of effort and made sacrifices, and you finally get to ride your efforts to the life you want. This book will place a lot of emphasis on this formula. The fact that this one method may help you and your family live the lifestyle you desire cannot be emphasized enough. It's not simple, but if you reach your financial objectives, the work and sacrifice will be worthwhile.

What you will discover at the book's conclusion.

The lessons you can gain from this book. a glossary of concepts, practical tips, and tools you can use to track and manage your money. You will have a thorough grasp of how to make money, save money, budget, invest, and a number of other subjects by the time you finish reading this book. This will serve as the cornerstone on which you may develop your personal finances and accumulate a net worth sufficient to support your current standard of living and provide your family the life they have always dreamed of.

Keep a notebook close by so you can jot down any phrases, ideas, or concepts that you wish to further study. You may come across things throughout this book that you want to learn more about. Your future success depends on your ability to learn and adapt. When your parents were starting their careers, if you told them what will be typical 30 years from now, they wouldn't believe you. The many modern conveniences we enjoy are a result of technological advancement and invention, and change is occurring more quickly than it did in the previous 30 years. As a result, being flexible, open to change, and fast to pick up new information can help you take advantage of professional, income-boosting, and family-related chances. This book won't be the end-all, be-all of learning; rather, it'll be the first step in the constant process of acquiring new knowledge.

Some More Advice

Please be a bit more patient if you're growing tired of reading about all these life lessons and ideas and want to read about some useful information. We have time for all those budgeting and money-saving suggestions, but more importantly, if you want your efforts to be effective, you must have the appropriate attitude and be able to cope with challenges. Check out these four pieces of wisdom that might save your life. Keep them in mind so you'll be prepared for similar situations.

Having Self-Belief
Your net worth demonstrates your self-worth, according to a well-known adage. The amount of money you have in your pockets greatly depends on how you see yourself. They start acting in a manner that allows them to pursue their objectives and boost their financial success because they are more confident in taking the actions that will get them there. This is all because they believe in themselves and recognize how much

they can accomplish. The reason we place such a strong emphasis on your financial attitude is because it all begins with having the appropriate frame of mind and self-belief.

According to studies, those who make a lot of money or have successful lives all have high levels of self-worth. These individuals all exude self-assurance and counsel others to do the same. Surprisingly, the majority of these affluent individuals previously believed they weren't competent or deserving enough to accomplish so much and become so wealthy. However, they had to overcome this obstacle before continuing on to lead fulfilling lives.

If you are still unsure about your ability to reach your financial objectives as you read this, you need to stop reading right now and make a definite choice. Make the decision to use all means necessary to achieve your goals and to do everything in your ability to achieve them.

Let's imagine for a second that you don't have confidence in your ability to succeed. Given that, it's likely that you doubt your ability to achieve financial success. If you have this belief, you won't take the necessary measures to become financially successful, such as saving money, investing it, consulting a financial counselor, or even reading this eBook. We are aware of your potential and your conviction that, with the right support, you can achieve your objectives. If you have any negative thoughts about yourself, you should modify them. The harder part is figuring out which ones they are. If you don't alter these unfavorable thoughts, you can act in ways that aren't healthy for you and might even make you feel worse about yourself!

Putting Your Family to Work

If you live alone, you may want to skip this chapter. However, if you want to get the most out of this eBook and live with your husband or wife and their family, you must read this section.

A car's four wheels propel it. What would happen if one wheel attempted to move the vehicle forward or even in the other direction while the other three were stuck? Not only will the automobile not go forward even a fraction of an inch, but the one wheel's attempt will harm both it and the rest of the car. This comparison nicely captures the scenario when one family member is attempting to handle their money wisely in order to improve their financial condition in the future, but the other family members are not supporting them. All of your efforts are really negated when your spouse, kids, or other family members do not make an attempt in the same direction as you, or when they actually do unfavorable financial actions. It might be wiser for you to give up altogether if your family is not on board. You will just cause yourself further stress and a waste of time, much as the odd wheel will harm itself while trying to pull the wheel ahead. What then is the answer?

As you read this eBook and get the financial knowledge you need, be sure that the rest of your family has reached the same level of financial literacy. You may suggest to your spouse that they read this eBook with you, or you could get your family together and have a meeting. You may impart to your family the crucial knowledge they need, such as prudent budgeting, saving, and spending. Effective communication of the following message is the aim: "I need my family's help to secure a better future for them by making informed and prudent financial decisions with the money we already have," I said.

You may take a number of actions to inform your family about their money. Meetings with family members, financial adviser appointments, life lessons, and so on. However, if you have this eBook, all you need to prepare yourself and your family on the path to success is the knowledge in this book and some talking. One option is to offer that your spouse read this eBook; if they are hesitant, you may suggest to them the particular chapters that you believe they should and are most knowledgeable about. If you're still having trouble getting them to read, try just talking to them about what you've discovered.

If your kids are old enough, you may ask them to read books about money. Although not all of the chapters in this eBook will be enjoyable or helpful for children, you may choose which ones they must read. It will be much simpler for you if your kids are too young to grasp this book. You're good to go if you include your kids in educational activities and lessons.

How to Handle Obstacles

It would be incorrect to assume that once you become financially educated, you won't experience loss ever again in your life since even the finest financial gurus and counselors out there make financial blunders and suffer from significant losses. Yes, you will reduce your likelihood of suffering future losses, but readiness and information can only get you so far. You are a person, and as a human, you will make mistakes sometimes. Therefore, be ready to clean up the mess if anything similar ever occurs. Although time cannot be turned back, there are certain things you can do to lessen the harm.

Don't Worry: You may be paving the way for even more financial difficulties in your life if you tend to overspend under stress or do financially risky actions in an effort to bounce back more quickly after a setback. When you're in a position like this, you should strive to put emotion out of the picture and look for a solution. Never ignore or disregard the error you committed, if any, in an attempt to make yourself feel better about the damages. Instead, you should acknowledge it and accept it with ease to avoid repeating. Put your attention on doable options, like finding a job to generate some more money or reducing your spending.

Seek Assistance: If you are under stress or finding it difficult to concentrate on what needs to be done to cope with a setback, you should seek quick assistance from dependable friends, family, or a professional adviser. Never be embarrassed to ask for help. Call a financial counselor or specialist on the phone and explain your situation to them. Remember that holding everything within your head and avoiding discussing the problem and possible solutions with others will only make you feel more stressed out emotionally.

Determine your losses A financial setback sometimes entails several losses or damages. These kinds of setbacks often consist of a number of lesser issues. Consequently, it is not a smart idea to try to take the situation by the horns. You must do a careful analysis of the circumstances and attempt to estimate your overall losses. You can only begin to formulate a recovery strategy after enumerating the damages. When presented with such a predicament, many individuals choose to keep themselves unconscious of their losses; they purposely keep themselves in the dark, yet doing so may only lead to greater strain and worry. Bring your losses into the open and expose the wounds. By doing this, regardless of how painful it may be, you will only have to feel the sting of your losses once. Instead of remaining depressed all the time and doing nothing to change your position, you may start recuperating after the injury has healed.

Be Consistent: Regardless of the severity of your loss, if you allow it to shake your commitment, you will just lose more. A financial setback might be considerably harder to recover from if you ignore your rules, current budget, and due payment dates. In order to save some money, review your costs and reevaluate your priorities. You'll find it simpler to restart saving as a result. It will help you cope with the stress and worry of the situation to reevaluate your budget and take proactive measures. Taking action will make you feel much better, even if the situation doesn't improve right away.

Take Care of Yourself: The adage, "Money is a tool, not a consequence," is even more true today. You must not let your issues to control you. Avoid being too stressed out and losing sleep. Avoid overindulging in either drinking or smoking. You can only act to change your position once you are in top physical and mental condition.

A contented person is wealthy.

You'll most likely get better counsel than this from nobody else, I think. Yes, you may have already heard it a thousand times. But have you really taken this counsel to heart and applied it to your everyday life? We have all heard the clichés "money doesn't buy happiness" and "money is only temporary" many times. Only a small minority of individuals genuinely believe and behave in this manner, however.

The relationship between wealth and happiness is significant. prosperous countries and prosperous individuals are, as they say, much happier than impoverished nations or communities, and this is a reality. You should be aware that, contrary to popular belief, money has less of an impact on happiness than you may assume. Having more money available to spend has a negligible impact on your happiness if you have access to shelter, clothing, and food.

Of sure, having money makes you happy, but how much happier? What about the other parts of the tale because we only have one piece of the puzzle? More money doesn't necessarily make you happier, as shown by studies and personal experience, but it might make your life even more unpleasant. It is not being suggested that you adopt a monastic lifestyle or stop caring about money in this instance. Balance is vital, not financial balance but mental balance. Even the poorest and wealthiest individuals may maintain happiness with the proper mental equilibrium.

Making Purchasing Choices

Let's take a minute to discuss the second significant risk to our financial stability: how to make purchasing choices. Making an accurate determination of whether something is a "need" or a "desire" is the first obstacle that every individual must overcome when making purchasing choices. Consider it this way to help you decide: If the item is needed, it is one that is covered by your survival budget. If not, it is only a wish. Let's maintain it that way because, in all honesty, understanding yourself in the most basic terms and your financial situation makes life so much simpler.

You need to grasp something, however, that you may not have heard previously. You're allowed to have wants! Yes, having desires is OK. You don't have to feel bad if you want cable TV, go out to eat, go on vacation, or any of those other things. The choices you make after realizing whether something is a necessity or a want are what matter here. Let's imagine, for instance, that all of your requirements are met (which should be the case before you decide on wants), and you now have the choice of increasing your savings or going on a date. The natural decision is to put the money into savings since, according to some, doing so is the most responsible course of action. But maybe the choice isn't as simple as it seems. If you take a close look at the circumstance, both choices are motivated by wants. Anything you do with this money is a want since it cannot be used to fulfill a need. Therefore, the actual question is, "What kind of life do you want to lead?" You may invest it in anything, increase your emergency savings cushion, or put that money into savings to perhaps save up for a bigger buy. Alternately, you may take the money and invest it in a memorable event that would enrich your life. The key here is that you must make a choice based on your knowledge of yourself and be OK with it going ahead in your life. The objective is not that one choice is correct and another is bad.

The idea of a "sale" is another part of purchasing choices. You need to be aware of a couple subtleties that are at play here. First off, just though you claimed to have "saved" $100 does not negate the fact that you just spent $200. Amounts paid out remain paid out. Second, and you may already be aware of this, businesses exploit the idea of a sale to persuade you that there is a deadline for purchasing that product or service at a discount. Have you ever seen a shop with a "going out of business" sign up all year long for the previous three years, for instance? How long does it take for a firm to close its doors? It's a strategy to incite consumers' F.O.M.O., or fear of missing out, to make a purchase. It's a time-tested method that has worked for ages and will continue to do so. You should pause at these points and consider if you are acting logically or emotionally while making a purchase. A good bargain will still be a good deal in 24 hours, according to wise folks. It's probably an emotional purchase choice if you can't wait 24 hours to decide. On the other hand, some individuals may hold off on making a purchase because they believe they will later come across a better offer, even if it pertains to something they really need. This is only another F.O.M.O. variant. When was the last time you purchased anything at an uncomfortable price, even if you needed it? If you believe this may be you. How long did it take you to finally make that choice? These are indicators that you're approaching purchasing choices with a different set of feelings than the individual who can't manage to wait 24 hours before making a purchase.

But let's reiterate that rationality, not passion, is the enemy in this situation. The adversary here is your ignorance about who you are and the motivations behind your choices. Consider that you find it difficult to wait a whole day before making a purchase. If you are aware of this about yourself, make financial preparations accordingly. Set aside a certain amount of "sale" money for emotional expenditures. Alternately, go shopping with a companion and instruct them to prevent you from making any purchases for the following 24 hours. Those of you who put off making purchases could benefit from having someone close by who prefers to make choices about purchases within 24 hours to assist persuade you to make the purchases that would really improve your life. You may also save money that you HAVE to spend in the next 24 hours, but that is a ridiculous concept. The important thing to remember is that now that you are aware of who you are, you can make plans and purchases that go along with who you are.

Review your financial situation in Chapter III.

FINANCIAL CONDITION

The ability of a person to acquire or get financial help is referred to as their financial standing. It may also be referred to as a person's capacity for survival. Most Americans' financial circumstances don't make it worthwhile. The Federal Reserve Board published a report on the economic well-being of American households on May 14, 2020. Despite the fact that this survey is normally performed annually, the Board agreed to conduct extra surveys in April and July 2020 as a result of the current pandemic. The report's goals were to assess the financial security of American households and identify the hazards to their finances. For many Americans, 2020 has been a stressful year. Numerous companies were forced to close as a result, which ultimately had an impact on many Americans' quality of life. One American out of every ten had to borrow money to cover everyday costs. Therefore, this year will serve as a year of lessons for Americans to develop a desire to save money. According to 46% of those polled as a whole, the pandemic's emergence made them better savers (Fox).

According to the CNBC report and the survey done using Survey Monkey about the causes Americans believed led to a decrease in their spending habits, 53% of people believe that the nation's economic situation is the main reason that they cut back on their spending and steered them toward saving. Losing a spouse who contributes to the family income was cited by 26% of Americans as the cause, which prompted them to reduce their spending. A stock market crisis is a danger to 16% of American respondents, and as a result, they reduce their expenditures. According to 14% of respondents, they began saving because they were concerned about losing their existing jobs. Medical costs for families increased throughout the epidemic, which ultimately helped to raise awareness of the need of conserving money. According to 9% of those being polled, high medical costs are what make them compromise on their spending, while 11% of respondents said that non-medical situations cause them to alter their priorities from spending to conserving. The description is summarized in the graph shown below.

Therefore, if Americans save more from their take-home pay than they actually spend, their financial situation tends to improve. A person's financial situation is determined by how financially secure they feel about themselves, whether from a professional or personal perspective. They should be able to handle any expenses without worry or pain. Everybody wants to reach a point in their financial lives where they feel safe and are able to easily and successfully fulfill all of their financial responsibilities. However, achieving such position requires unending concessions and sacrifices. We sometimes see things from very different perspectives. Imagine a little youngster operating a fancy vehicle. According to what we hear, the child is clearly wasting his father's money on high-end vehicles. On the other hand, the boy's father can have a personal account of how he fought and tried hard to save his kids the same fate. Therefore, one's financial situation may influence another's impulse or want to enjoy life's pleasures without any constraints. However, it is advised that one consider their financial situation before pursuing someone to get the stuff they possess. Examining one's financial situation can help one develop the ability to regulate their spending, which will ultimately enable them to set spending limits that are in line with their income.

CONTROL YOUR DEBT

In the first quarter of 2019, Americans reported having a $13.95 trillion debt (Staff, 2019). The borrowers borrow enormous sums of money from banks and financial institutions as interest rates start to drop. The borrower's capacity to make simple and feasible installment payments increases with decreasing interest rates. They often overlook this, however, if their salary enables them to save money for payments. The lower interest rate causes inflation because, in the end, if everyone has easy access to a house and a car, the increased demand will have an impact on the supply of that thing, which will raise the price of that thing. The two debt kinds most prevalent in America are either home debt or student loans. Despite the American government's initiative to introduce FPUC, the recent pandemic resulted in a massive increase in unemployment that had an impact on Americans' lifestyles, forced them to shoulder a debt burden, and ultimately led to them consulting various financial institutions across the nation.

Debt Management Techniques

We already spoke about the factors to take into account that motivate us to manage our debt. The first choice we have is to load ourselves with debt in order to fund a necessity. Instead of borrowing the whole amount from the financial institution, if one has previously saved a specific amount of money, he will have some to contribute. People incur debt because they believe it to be the simplest method to escape any situation. They like it, too. These folks, however, are unaware that it would take a decade or two for them to be debt-free. The following tactics may be used to assist you pay off your debt. One must always begin somewhere, and the first step to managing debt is to refrain from taking on more debt. It just takes one debt to get started. Most individuals develop the habit of going to the bank to borrow money whenever they run into financial difficulties. The first thing to avoid is this. Avoid adding to your stress and remain calm. If you need money, consider other options including renting out a room, cutting spending, looking for paying visitors, and working a part-time job to cover costs and prevent taking on further debt.

Instead of raising the number of payments, you may instead raise the amount of each installment to escape financial problems. This is a helpful strategy, but if you succeed, you will quickly be debt-free. Avoid using credit cards if you are living paycheck to paycheck since they are the cause of rising expenses and when the bill comes due at the end of the month, you have nowhere to turn. Your efforts to get the cash necessary to pay your credit card bills finally prove unsuccessful, and you are subject to penalties that must be paid at a later date. Utilizing your retirement funds to pay off debt or, if you have any, liquidating an insurance policy are two further debt management strategies. In an emergency, it is better to utilize retirement money and insurance policies than to approach a bank for a loan.

Instead of focusing all of your energy and life on repaying the debt, we should start thinking creatively. The most wholesome kind of economy is one where money is actively being circulated. A sound economy produces a solid social structure with high standards and sincere behavior. Therefore, as Americans, we should think large and best rather than keeping money in our wallets. An educated individual looks for possibilities wherever they can find them. Our goal is to find ways to produce white revenue for both our own well-being and the well-being of our nation. As is common knowledge, income is a need for survival. As was previously said, we constantly search for investment options. Saving a little money now can ensure a happy future. Short-term income is an income that enables an individual to generate a steady stream of cash flow for bill payment and further investment. Investment has a short-term effect. Small investments, such as purchasing stock in a particular firm or purchasing bonds that pay interest to investors, may be used to earn short-term income. As a result, income from dividends and interest increases a person's capacity to cover certain expenses. The periodic generation of short-term income results in immediate and short-term financial flows. The short-term income might be advantageous for both commercial organizations and individuals. Business entities engage in stock trading activities to cover costs such as bill payments and enhance the company's marketing efforts. Despite the fact that dividends from stocks and shares create revenue. These dividend-paying stocks have a better rate of return than bonds, but they also carry a higher level of risk. As a result, if a shareholder of a short-term security notices that the stock he owns is rising in value, he may sell it for a profit while still receiving a greater level of principle protection. A person may repay a loan's installment with short-term income; they can also use it to make a down payment on a home or car loan, for example.

When it comes to long-term income, the situation is a little different. Long-term investments provide long-term income. One must consistently retain the investing instrument or product for a longer amount of time while making a long-term investment. To generate significant long-term income, one must develop patience and refrain from selling an asset or instrument as soon as they become aware of its declining worth. People looking to generate long-term income invest mostly in stocks, bonds, and derivatives with maturities longer than one year.

MONITOR YOUR SPENDING

A person must first define their aim in order to determine which direction to travel in and what action to take, whether to invest in short-term securities or long-term assets. The best option for him if he wants to advance gradually is a short-term investment, and if he wants to sit back and hold the asset for longer than a year, he should either get a yield on it in the form of interest or a dividend, or in the case of a fixed asset, sell it in the market to reap the greatest rewards, as soon as the asset reaches maturity. The fruit will be sweeter and more profitable the longer someone waits. The choice of investment, however, is based on your savings or the amount you have available to purchase or invest in such assets. Keeping an eye on your expenditures should be your first priority. If a person doesn't know where all of their money goes or where they've spent their income, how can they regulate their spending? Saving money is the answer to everything. What is being frugal? Thriftiness is the phrase for being thrifty with your money. People who are thrifty and frugal think twice before making large purchases. The best strategies for Americans to keep track of numerous of their spending must be understood. The priority is following the account history. The majority of

Americans use plastic money to make purchases. However, a small portion of the population finds it difficult to keep track of their purchases. Even while keeping receipts in our pockets may seem like a hassle, they are useful for monitoring our daily or monthly expenses and for determining which items are the most expensive in terms of both cost and usefulness.

Online, there are many different budgeting templates to choose from. These templates are essentially spreadsheets that enable users to record the costs of the goods that correspond to their purchases before totaling the costs. These spreadsheets are useful for reducing unforeseen costs that are hard on the wallet.

The creation of software that is accessible to both Android and iOS users is a top priority for mobile application developers. These tools provide customers a platform to track their expenditure, list it down, and decide which expenses to reduce. Some apps are free, while others need payment. Everyone appreciates free apps since they don't need a monthly or yearly membership charge, yet these apps are unreliable. The majority of the time, a pop-up advertising interrupts the process of capturing the data. There's a risk you'll overlook something as well. Therefore, if you want to keep track of your spending on portable devices like smartphones, iPads, tablets, etc., it is advised to get some budgeting software. Dollarbird, Fudget, Mint, Mvelops, Personal Capital, Penny, etc. are a few well-known programs.

According to studies, when our income rises, we spend more since our comfort levels rise as well. We could think a little home is too small and long for a larger one, just as we might think our current automobile is too small. We search for larger and more opulent goods because we feel that the automobiles we now own don't appear to live up to our standards. We neglect to live within our means, and as a consequence, we are affected by the inflation of living. You escape this lifestyle inflation via gratitude and modesty. Utilizing maid services for tasks like laundry, sweeping, and dishwashing is another expenditure that may damage your savings strategy and has to be monitored. As a result, it is advised that you engage in self-work.

Most of the time, we go out window shopping intending to purchase nothing, but we end up purchasing a variety of items. This interferes with your effort to save money. To reduce the arbitrary costs you could incur when window shopping, monitoring your spending carefully might assist. Any small bit of money saved from a paycheck helps a person build a successful fortune.

Effects of the Epidemic on American Consumer Spending

According to 64% of Americans, the pandemic's escalation has caused them to prioritize conserving money above purchasing. A poll was done by the Bank of America in early September 2020. The group polled more than 2,500 American individuals. Many individuals lost their jobs as a result of the epidemic, which had an influence on how they lived before. Many individuals were able to avoid losing their jobs thanks to technology, since ethical businesses allowed their staff to work from home. Undoubtedly, not all businesses could afford the pricey equipment needed to link workers' homes to their workstations' IP addresses. Therefore, the only thing they had done to avoid incurring significant costs was to terminate the superfluous workers. The difficulty level, nevertheless, was the same for those who had the benefit of having their hob secured, but the degree of difficulty was a little less intense. During the epidemic, those who worked from home were able to save the cost of commuting. People were unable to dine out because of the strict lockdowns, which tends to reduce the cost of eating. While the epidemic undoubtedly lowered expenditures, it also led to greater misery and poverty. People who lost their employment due to the epidemic had no choice but to use what little money they had saved up to cover their basic expenses.

Finders Keepers

The one thing you have known your whole life that you must do to take care of your money is to hang onto it. The most effective approach to show yourself and everyone around you that you are in charge of your money, have a healthy regard for it, and maintain as much of it as you can is to keep as much of it as you can. After reading this section, many individuals will claim they cannot afford to save. Can you really state that you cannot afford to save after carefully going through your budget plan and examining your financial situation? This is not meant to imply that you are not having trouble making ends meet, but rather to ask what behaviors could be keeping you from setting aside some money each month. You are really aggravating the problem since you are unable to save any money each month.

Saving even a little amount is preferable than doing nothing at all. Start small and rise through the ranks.

One of the most important behaviors to develop over time can drastically alter your financial outlook is this one. First, pay yourself. Although it may seem like a fairly basic piece of advice, it may be one of the most effective habits you ever form. Pay a portion of your monthly paycheck as soon as it is received into a separate account that is used only for investing and savings. Don't tamper with what you paid for. Consider it like a mortgage payment. Although you would never think of skipping it, once it has been paid, you are not allowed to get it back. This calls for self-control and action, but if you establish a monthly pattern, it becomes a part of your routine, and eventually, you won't hesitate to take this step.

You should try to set aside at least 10% of your monthly income as self-pay each month. I can already hear you gasping for air and hating me for proposing such a ridiculous amount to set aside each month, but no one ever claimed managing your finances or your money would be simple. To achieve the results you want, discipline, consistent excellent habits, and action are necessary. However, it is more than feasible and attainable. To start the process, save aside simply 1% of your monthly income. You'll quickly come to understand that saving only 1% of your income in a separate account is doable, and you'll be able to adjust to living off the other 99% of your income. As you get the hang of saving 1% of your paycheck each month, raise it to 2%, then 3%, and so forth until you hit the 10% goal you're aiming for. The exponential growth of your savings will become apparent to you over time, which will inspire you to continue saving and preserving as much of your money as you can. You will be motivated to start acting right away and establishing this monthly habit just by doing some simple arithmetic.

Let's say that your monthly pay is £1000 after taxes. Sorry for stating the obvious, but you pay yourself first 10% of your monthly salary, or £100. This amounts to £1200 over the course of a year. The total payment over ten years is £12,000. The original £12,000 funding you collected is utilized to fund investments and savings accounts along the road, which provide higher returns. You get the picture. I do not claim to be a financial expert, and I would always urge you to obtain independent financial advice before making an investment. Do you not feel motivated to pay yourself first after reading this? If you knew your money was working for you rather than against you, how much better would your life and the decisions you make be?

Use of a piggy bank is another behavior I heartily advise you to think about adopting since it may be done right now. I did really say a piggy bank. You may take a few minutes to compose yourself after laughing so hard at the piggy bank you painted at a kids' party when you were five years old and kept it in your bedroom. Okay, so although it may not be the most sophisticated way to save money, it works. I advise you to get a piggy bank that you must break to pieces in order to access your money rather than one that is simple to reach and obtain the money you placed into it. Again, discipline is the key to success here. There is no need to buy a piggy bank you have to break into if you are certain you won't touch the money inside. Instead, choose the choice that will work best for you after making sure you are developing the habit.

I just store £1 and £2 coins in them to truly understand how much money you can save utilizing the piggy bank approach. A £5 note is sometimes inserted. You will also realize how much money some of these bad boys can store once you start saving a little bit more than the tiny change most people typically keep in them. You may easily save £500 or more in a matter of weeks. You might use this money for enjoyable expenses like vacations or lunches out, or if you're very motivated to save at this stage, you can put it back into the separate account you use to pay yourself first. The idea is that it's yet another fantastic technique to save money you never believed you could. Try it out!

Save More Money

Setting up money is the first and most important thing to remember during harsh times! Spend as little as is reasonably possible, and put as much money in the bank as you can! Although it may seem like straightforward advice, an emergency might cause individuals to overreact.

Avoid attempting to pay as many invoices as you can! Assuming you pay for what is necessary, think about how long you can prolong your continuing assets. Make a list of the solicitations you should respond to right now and those you should postpone or decline.

You should deposit every dollar you save into your bank account. However, keep in mind that leaking roofs and malfunctioning gearboxes also have a timeline. You may need to use your stockpiles as a backup plan if you suddenly have a large charge.

The three basic methods for saving money that you may try are included in this article. While waiting, you might think about the following suggestions, which may help you save money more quickly and efficiently:

Make additional shopping excursions with family. You wouldn't believe how regularly a better offer may be found online or at a different shop.

Purchase a lot of mostly long-lasting food and household goods.

Cook more and order takeout less. Online, you may find many delicious recipes that cost very little money. Before you go for the store, evaluate them.

Having a kitchen garden is another way to keep your expenses under control. You have a variety of options when choosing one. By diverting the money from your basic food purchases to your investing accounts or other needs, you may lower the cost of doing so.

Get Security

Although the recent events were an unparalleled global health disaster, susceptibility may manifest itself in a variety of ways. However, much as during the pandemic, health problems and the passing of caregivers are the most common occurrences that worry families a great deal.

People need to select a good life, and health insurance plans should be used to prepare for this since they are essential for helping people deal with unforeseen crises both during and outside of pandemics. Without protection, people and their kin are helpless. Choosing protection plans that safeguard the whole family is essential.

You won't need to modify your way of life if your company is safe and you have enough health insurance for you and your family.

Have a hidden stash

It is essential to have a windy day for emergencies and erratic situations. When circumstances are favorable, conserving money and accumulating a hidden hoard is strongly advised. If your salary is suddenly cut off due to illness, loss of work, or other uncontrollable circumstances, you will have resources for your regular family expenses if you have a just-in-case account with 3-6 months' worth of expenses.

These resources might serve as a safety net when things are difficult. Create a monthly automated transfer of assets from current to investing accounts to make sure you're consistently building up your emergency savings.

Similarly, when things are tough, you could come up with creative ways to boost your emergency funds. Start by investing a portion of the money you were able to save by decreasing expenses, as described above.

Then, go through your closet, carport, and store for gently worn or unused items to sell on local Facebook groups or online ads. Small kitchen items, sporting equipment, and occasion attire are other viable options.

Guidelines For Managing Your Money Flow

With a few helpful hints and tried-and-true methods, you can effectively manage your cash flow. The majority of these suggestions are generic, but by adhering to them, you may master money management on your own.

Create a budget - You must create a budget based on all of your spending and then work to reduce them as required. A monthly budget is usually a smart idea.

Spend less than you make – This may seem obvious, but for some individuals, it is the root of all their financial problems. The cornerstone of sound financial management is this. You must create a spending plan that is less than your overall revenue.

Have an emergency money on hand; this is necessary for a backup plan. If an emergency arises, you may withdraw a little amount from the fund and then pay it back again to maintain your finances in tact. This emergency fund will provide financial stability in the event of any dire circumstances.

Shopping is a necessary evil, but it is possible to organize your purchases properly. Look for the greatest deals on the items you wish to purchase, and attempt to complete your shopping using discounts and rebates. For early notice of their promotional offers, you may sign up with your favorite stores using loyalty cards. Going for homemade meals is always preferable than dining out regularly. Compared to restaurant and takeout food options, homemade meals are not only cheaper but also healthier.

Use your credit card responsibly. You have a credit card, but you shouldn't use it sometimes to make purchases. It's easy to see why. The money must be paid with interest at a later date. When you have cash on hand, use your credit card to make a purchase since you may pay it off in 2-3 payments or after 45–50 days without incurring any interest. You may choose an interest-free EMI tied to a credit card to buy expensive things. The price may be paid in instalments without incurring interest. Instead, you may put the cost into a savings account.

Choose based on quality, not necessarily on name. Occasionally, test items from department shops that are not branded but have a reputation for high quality. This also applies to domestic goods, however it is best to avoid using this general guideline when it comes to food and cosmetics.

Recognize your error and spend some time reviewing your spending. Stop for a minute if you see any anomalies in your cost pattern. After reviewing the cost, start the self-clarification process. Really, do you need to purchase these? Think about the advantages and disadvantages.

Try to put aside at least 10 to 20 percent of your income as savings. Maintain this cash in a bank account. When you have some money saved up, invest it in a financial plan.

Modify your daily routine. Simple lifestyle adjustments might help you save money. Use your electrical equipment, for instance, carefully. Practice yoga, bodyweight exercises, and free-hand movements at home instead of joining a gym. Instead of buying or renting DVDs from a DVD library or online movie streaming services, consider becoming a member.

Get Your Finances In Order

When there is a lot of paperwork involved, organizing funds might seem to be quite difficult. But if one's finances are structured, taking control of them is considerably simpler.

Select a system.

What kind of system one wants to choose is the first thing that a person must pick. Pen and paper is the simplest approach. Get a binder and label the sections with headings like "bills," "loan," "food," "donations," and "medical funds." There is no ideal level of spending since it might vary depending on one's priorities. Additionally, there are web-based tools available to monitor cash flow.

Bills must be arranged.

Make sure the mail is packaged in one sizable envelope for delivery. Lost invoices might result in delinquent accounts and late payments. Sort the banknotes into different groups. All the electrical bills in one file may be grouped together as one bill, or the bills can be grouped by month. This will make it simpler for someone to review their spending from the previous month.

Pay your bills on time.

Up to 10 billings may be sent to a home per month. Decide when you will pay all of these expenses at once. Make sure to plan your schedule so that no bills are due late. A person will spend too much time in front of the checkbook if they pay the bill as often as they get it. Remember that there is always a grace period for paying debts. To find out when the payment is due and avoid being labeled late, contact the creditor.

Benefit from Automatic Payments

Almost all banks provide a feature that allows customers' accounts to be automatically debited for payments to creditors. Additionally, since using this service enables borrowers to get their funds more quickly, most creditors would cut their interest rates for such borrowers. Just be careful to maintain track of these deductions to monitor financing and prevent checks being bouncing.

Enroll in Direct Deposit

Payroll is credited to a person's immediately accessible account via direct deposit. This kind of revenue may be established quickly and is much simpler to monitor. Additionally, people should ensure that they obtain a pay stub from their employment that details all of the period's deductions.

Close Inactive Accounts

Unused accounts should be cancelled. Send a formal letter asking them to close it to the bank or credit card company. This will enhance credit standing and serve as a practical means of preventing inadvertent expenditure. When salespeople attempt to entice you with reduced interest rates, resist the urge to create a new account.

Combined Accounts

Make an effort to combine numerous credit cards into one. Check the interest rates and the balance transfer. The trouble of dealing with a lot of paperwork may be avoided by keeping money in a few locations.

Put Automatic Savings in Place

Establish a connection between your checking and savings accounts so that money will be automatically transferred from the regular account to the savings account. Each month, this is accomplished via bank services. Savings will grow more quickly if you start a savings deposit.

Expenses in Chapter 3: How to Restrict Your Spending

On a tight budget, people desire limitless things. One frequent issue is spending money on things we don't need. Keeping costs under control is simple if you give it enough attention.

Using less electricity

Lowering the consumer's power bill is a perk of energy conservation. One may cut their power use without spending a lot of money.

Improve the house's insulation. Consumer data suggest that closing the seams in the home might cut usage by 30%. To fill gaps around the doors and windows, get caulk and weatherstripping.

At night, use heat generators. Use heat-intensive equipment like the oven and dryer at night, when it's colder outside. Using heat-generating equipment throughout the day will make the air conditioner work harder to maintain a cool temperature.

Use cold water to wash your clothes. A family would save at least $152 a year if they wash their clothing in cold water.

Use a slow cooker. Slow cookers use less energy and don't raise the indoor temperature.

Dry clothes outside. Establish a routine of drying your clothing outdoors or in a spare room. Avoid immediately exposing clothes that have been dried in the sun to heat as this might fade the colors. Hangers may be used to dry clothing indoors.

Fan the flames. Try switching to electric fans instead of using air conditioners on days when it's not all that warm.

Turn off all electronics. One of the greatest methods to limit electricity usage is via this. When no one is home, flip the main switch off.

Monthly air filter replacement. Filters that are dirty may limit airflow, which makes the system work harder.

Advice on Cutting Food Costs

The secret to reducing food costs without compromising nutrition is to go to the store prepared. Here are some tips to assist someone save money while shopping.

Don't use the prepared mix. Bagged salad mixes may be practical, but they may be expensive and soon go bad. Instead, purchase lettuce since it usually lasts longer.

Develop your own. If someone has adequate room in their backyard, they should think about producing their own vegetables. Only a few bucks can buy a package of seeds.

buy a lot of spices. Spices are essential components for maintaining the flavor and health of food. Look for businesses that offer spices in bulk since they are sometimes less expensive.

Cut costs on basics. When they are on sale, buy essentials like canned foods and cooking oil.

fond of potatoes. A excellent source of fiber, vitamin C, and potassium is the potato. They may be used in a variety of cuisines and are quite adaptable.

Choose chicken. Chicken is more affordable and healthier than beef. Purchase them while they're discounted and like roasting them.

Add beans for bulk. People who want to put on weight should try eating beans as they are fairly affordable and high in protein and fiber. Include them in stir-fries and salads.

whole grains. Brown rice, barley, and whole-wheat pizza are affordable whole grain options.

Purchase ground beef. Due to its primary component, ground beef, meatloaf is renowned for being affordable. Lean meat is the healthier option.

Be aware of seafood offers. A person's risk of heart disease may be lowered by eating seafood at least twice a week. Look for promotions in the fish area. Fish that is frozen is often less costly.

fish in cans. Additionally, canned tuna has the essential omega-3 fatty acids that may support heart health. Also less expensive than fresh or frozen fish is canned seafood.

Invest in frozen veggies. Because they are harvested at the height of ripeness and frozen to retain their nutrients, frozen veggies are healthful.

Advice for Shopping Cheap Clothes

Clothing is an integral aspect of everyday living. Budget harm might result from the ongoing need to keep up with the latest fashions. Here are some suggestions on how to look good and save money.

Purchase with cash. The simplest method to prevent this from happening is to just purchase reasonably priced clothing. If someone doesn't have the money to purchase the clothing they desire, they should start saving.

Shop at outlet stores. People may shop at discount retailers for fashionable clothing. Don't overfill the trolley and pay attention to the products.

Go shopping off-season. Seasonal clothing tends to be more costly, so purchase winter jackets in the spring and summer garments in the winter.

Look for discounts online. For coupons, subscribe to newsletters. This is a terrific way to stay up to date on the most recent discounts.

Don't simply purchase anything because it is inexpensive. Keep in mind that not everyone will find what they are seeking for right away. Don't give in to the urge to purchase the clothing just because it is on sale. Only invest in apparel that you are certain to wear.

Accessorize. A person may completely alter their appearance by just changing their accessories.

Budgeting and Maintaining Fitness

Even while individuals are beginning to search for methods to save costs, they should never sacrifice their own health. Here are some cheap ways to remain active.

Personal training on steroids. A personal trainer is required to set up an efficient exercise regimen by instructing a person in new movements while maintaining perfect form. A less expensive option is to enroll in small group training sessions where participants may share the cost and get guidance from a trainer.

YMCA. The YMCA offers its members a full range of swimming and exercise facilities. Additionally, the majority of branches provide discounts to families.

Working out burns calories. Try to ride a bike or walk to work. The metabolism may also be boosted in the morning by doing this.

Boot training on the playground. Make a customized boot camp out of a few pieces of wood and some car tires. This can be a fun, inexpensive way to train.

Bring your kids. Go for a stroll or a bike ride in the park with the kids to spend some quality time together. To get them moving, plan some trekking excursions sometimes.

Construct a home gym. There are benefits to exercising at home. It provides greater privacy and is much more practical. A person doesn't need a lot of tools. Resistance bands, a yoga mat, skipping ropes, and a stability ball are some of the less expensive pieces of equipment.

Benefit from the weekend. Make it a habit to work out by going back to the fundamentals at least once a week. Swimming, biking, and hiking are all free activities.

Become close over a rush. Replace an expensive night out with friends with a cheap exercise. When done in a group, staying in shape may become a social activity.

Budget-friendly Luxuries to Enjoy

Budgeting for one's needs does not require giving up all of life's luxuries. Everyone should be able to enjoy and take pleasure in the activities they choose, and doing so doesn't have to be expensive.

masseuse at home. Everybody should unwind and indulge in a massage sometimes. Most individuals only get them as a special treat since they may cost up to $70 at a salon. An inexpensive solution is to buy a vibrating belt or foot massager.

Dogs. Man's best buddy is a title given to dogs for a reason. These K-nines make the ideal companion and have been shown to lower anxiety and tension. Instead of buying a dog from a breeder, try to adopt one and provide it with a second home.

Local travel. Flying across the globe might be enjoyable, but it can cost the average individual their whole lifetime's savings. Stay close to home and visit museums and historical places instead.

Prosecco. Italian wine called prosecco is a wonderful substitute for champagne. These are often under $10 a bottle.

Unique jewelry. Although handcrafted jewelry might appear excessive and pricey, Etsy, an online store that focuses on handmade items, often has fantastic discounts. Even special requirements might be fulfilled by the shopkeepers.

It's like to having your very own personal jeweler.

Film night. Try to watch TV along with some friends one night. A home TV may provide a different viewing experience than a big screen, but individuals at home are freer to yell, laugh, and chat as much as they choose.

Facials. You may also do spa services like facials at home. Simply get a face pack and spa salt from a department shop and use them at home.

How To Maintain Focus

It might be challenging to overcome lifelong spending patterns after deciding to make a personal budget and live within your means. Here are some suggestions to help you keep on track toward meeting your financial goal and staying within your budget.

• Make a cash payment. One of the easiest ways to stick to your spending limit is to do this. Set a weekly budget for how much you will need to spend, withdraw the necessary amount of cash from your account to cover your costs, and then promise yourself that you will not be able to spend any more money until the following week. By doing this, you'll be able to control yourself and get rid of your reliance on credit cards. You won't be tempted to buy more than you can afford if you just use cash.

- Quit vices and other undesirable behaviors. Small everyday costs that you are unaware are really mounting up over time are one of the ways you wind up spending too much without realizing it. For instance, if you consume one can of soda every day, you may be surprised to see how much it truly costs you over the course of a month or a year. The same holds true for any other unhealthy habits you could have, like smoking or drinking alcohol. Calculate how much you spend each month on booze or cigarettes, then consider how much you might save if you saved that money instead of squandering it. Weaning yourself off of these vices also has the vital side benefit of helping your health.
- Collaborate with your partner or other family members. If everyone in the family contributes, staying within a budget is simpler. Therefore, it would be beneficial if you get down to make a

budget with your husband and family. To define how much each family member should spend, you may, for instance, make a spending plan. Then, you could have regular weekly meetings to assess your progress. However, it's also crucial to identify solutions with family members who seem to be struggling to stick to their own spending limits rather than criticizing them.

• Continue keeping an eye on your spending. Even after you've made the decision to make a personal budget, it's crucial to maintain track of your spending. Without ongoing awareness of where your money is going, there is a chance that you may relapse and trouble areas will start to reappear. Simply preserve the receipts for your purchases so that you may analyze them later if you feel the need to do so and find areas of spending leakage. You don't need to be too obsessive and meticulous about it.

Alternately, you may start a spending journal where you record your purchases in a notebook so you can look back on them later.

- Arrange your costs in advance to prevent irrational spending. For instance, always remember to write a list before you leave the house for the grocery store or the mall. This will serve as a reminder of what you need to acquire as well as a tool for controlling your expenditures.
- Consider if you absolutely need something or whether you can wait to get it before making any significant purchases. Additionally, consider if you can have anything you currently possess reconditioned or mended rather than purchasing something new.
- If you have had a significant shift in your life, review your tax withholding. This will assist in confirming the accuracy of the amount you are stating.

Remember that if your withholding is insufficient, you will owe more taxes in April. However, if it's too large, you'll be giving the government an interest-free loan for a whole year even though the money may be repaid as a tax refund. Set aside money for unforeseen costs. There will always be moments when you spend more money than you intended to or exceed your budget. When these things occur, don't be too harsh on yourself; instead, make a commitment to improve going forward. If you punish yourself or become too angry, you could decide to give up on your budget because you think you won't be able to keep to it.

Money Management Best Tips

Things might be challenging for college students at times, particularly when it comes to managing their finances. With all the coursework you already have to do, creating a budget with school fees and other costs might be a bother. However, if you follow these easy steps, you will be able to manage your money with ease.

1. The first thing you may do to start the process is to open a bank account. Most banks provide free account setup for college students, specifically for these types of accounts.

2. In addition to setting up your accounts, you may make a budget that lists all of your monthly spending, your allowances (if any), and your earned money. Use an online personal financial management application like https://www.mint.com, which enables

you to simply build and keep to a budget, to manage your spending and monitor your budget.

3. Only use your credit card in an emergency. You may have to pay a fee to use it or them. Even if getting a credit card and beginning to develop credit early is a good thing, it is encouraged to use it (or them) sparingly, if at all.

4. By purchasing old books or, if available, downloading books online, you may avoid going over your allotted spending limit on books. By doing this, you may decrease your spending in half and spend the money on other crucial school-related expenses.

5. Another effective strategy for preventing excessive spending is to set financial boundaries. Budgeting can help you choose if an expensive laptop or

smartphone is worthwhile when the time comes.

Although paying for college might be difficult, you can learn to manage your money responsibly and begin preparing yourself for future challenges that will be more difficult.

Advice on managing money (for a single person)

Being single sometimes might be a bit intimidating since you don't have any significant obligations, like a kid, and you can spend too much money. These easy procedures might assist in keeping you in charge of your financial management.

1. Stop making impulsive purchases. Just because you have money on hand doesn't mean you may spend it anyway you want. Try setting a budget and saving money for it if you find something you really want to purchase. In this manner, you will still have money in your savings after you purchase them.

2. Have a strategy in place. Making a strategy will undoubtedly be helpful while you're single. If you are able to save money up front, you will have more than enough saved to aid if anything goes wrong later on.

3. Although the following step could seem or sound absurd, it really poses a serious problem, particularly for singles. Learning to cook may cut down on a lot of unnecessary expenditure. Unexpectedly, you find yourself spending a lot of money at fast food establishments because you do not see the need to cook because you would only

be cooking for yourself, so it is no longer a priority. However, consider how much money you could save if you bought and cooked food that you could use another day rather than spending money every single day.

4. Retirement savings are a must for each stage of money management. Whether or whether you are in excellent health, you still need to start saving money for a rainy day.

5. Even if you don't have children or anybody else dependent on you, getting life insurance is still a smart financial move. You may be wondering why it has to be obtained. Consider it from this perspective: Would your family be able to cover the costs if you were sick tomorrow? What if you passed away? Would your family be able to cover the cost of your burial? Now that you understand my premise, you know it makes sense to get life insurance.

Advice on managing money (for married people)

Marriage is a beautiful thing, but there are times when tensions about money arise. These tensions ultimately lead to a rupture and divorce. You and your spouse will be placed on the road to financial success by the advice you are about to read.

1. There are various things that the two of you will need to address before the big proposal and before you answer yes, one of which is your money. This way, if any of you have debts or other obligations, you may work together to find the best solution. It is beneficial to discuss spending goals and restrictions.

2. Decide if you two will create joint bank accounts or maintain and use the

individual ones you now have. Combining accounts may be simpler in certain cases since you will save money on interest fees levied by the banks and will eventually strengthen your marriage because you will both have access to the accounts whenever you want to use them or check on them.

3. Setting up a budget is something we do at home, and this point cannot be emphasized enough. Having a budget is one thing; adhering to it is another. It gets simple after a few rounds, and it is certain that you will be able to save some money each month or whenever you are paid for labor. Although it requires patience and discipline, this will eventually become the norm.

4. Every area of money management must include retirement savings. It gets harder and harder to manage money as we age. Sometimes, it's not a matter of overspending or failing to stick to a

budget, but rather the fact that the economy is always changing and, to be fair, some of your salaries aren't, which leads you to spend more than you should. Avoid starting off with a lot of money to guarantee that you can save for retirement. Since retirement is already some years away, you may start modest with your savings. Even a tiny sum can soon add up and grow over time.

5. If one of you has debt, you and your spouse will need to discuss the best strategies to pay it off and keep it off. Even though it might be challenging and time-consuming, your marriage will feel less stressed after you are debt-free. You won't have to worry about it as much, and you can both speak about other topics like house ownership.

www.ingramcontent.com/pod-product-compliance
Lightning Source LLC
Chambersburg PA
CBHW050253120526
44590CB00016B/2335